UNSHACKLED

Life Changing Poetic Illustrations

By Carolyn Folston Martin

authorHOUSE™

1663 LIBERTY DRIVE, SUITE 200
BLOOMINGTON, INDIANA 47403
(800) 839-8640
WWW.AUTHORHOUSE.COM

First published by AuthorHouse 11/29/05

ISBN: 1-4259-0681-8 (e)
ISBN: 1-4208-6680-X (sc)
ISBN: 1-4208-6681-8 (dj)

Printed in the United States of America
Bloomington, Indiana

This book is printed on acid-free paper.

In Memory of My Father, Raleigh Folston, Sr.

In Honor of my mother, Geneva Folston
My Husband, Kevin Martin, Sr.
My children, Kelsee and Kevin Martin, Jr.
My brother and sister-in-law, Raleigh and Ruby Folston
and my sister Claudia

Foreword

I sincerely hope that, as you read this book, you'll experience a freedom beyond your ability to perceive or understand. I hope that you indeed become, unshackled. I've entitled this book, "Unshackled" because I believe that chains of bondage, be they physical, financial, mental or spiritual, will be broken as you meditate on these poetic illustrations. The poetic illustrations are written from the viewpoint of many of life's negative and positive experiences that we all share. I've prayed a great deal as I wrote these poems that God would speak through me as I speak to you in poetic form. Be blessed as you read them and remember that Jesus can create new life in you and cause you to become unshackled from a life of sin and dismay. He will give you new hope and inspire you to live a life full of abundance in every area of your life, every day of your life. I've included quite a few poems for the youth and teenagers too. I believe that these poems will cause them to think about their present activities and have a positive inspiration on their future destiny. It is my intention to influence them to allow Christ to take over their lives and allow Him to live through them for the rest of their lives.

I pray that these poetic illustrations will minister to people everywhere. I know that poetry can be positively enticing but also that enticing words have been used to destroy, in many cases, in our society. On the other hand, the word of God breaks the yoke of bondage and sets the captive free.

Table of Contents

The Pit

I saw some unusual creatures
Down in a pit one day
And as I watched their glaring eyes
They began to say

Why not come and join us
You should not delay
If you desire to do so
We'll show you the way

As you get up in the morning
And prepare to go on your way
Let evil thoughts corrupt your mind
Think on every negative thing
That you can find

You see, just think about it
Why should you be glad
You still haven't accomplished
Many things that you wished you had

That should make you angry
That should make you mad
You should experience great anxiety
And ultimately be very sad

I tried to quiet these doomed
Voices that echoed in my head
But they belligerently got louder
And ignored my wishes instead

Just think about it
They continued to go on
If you allow us to live
Through you, you'll
Become very strong

You can go about destroying
Lives just as we do
You can experience dark ventures
Instead of ones that acknowledge the truth

You can smile a deceiving smile
To people that you meet
You can backstab and cause
Confusion and tremendous
Turmoil wreak

Don't listen to any voices
That may come from the word
They're the most ridiculous
Ones that we have ever heard

You will become so powerful
As you worship our dark Lord
And in the end you will end
Up in the pit with us
A dark servant's reward

Satan, I bind you up
In the name of Jesus
I began to shout
The creatures drew back
And instantly all ran out

This vision has helped
Me tremendously to arm
Myself each day

It's taught me not to
Meditate on negative things
And to renew my mind each day

It's taught me how Satan plans
My life to destroy
That there's nothing more in
The world that he would enjoy

It's taught me to keep my
Eyes on Jesus so that negative
Things will not overpower me
That also by keeping my
Eyes on Him that I can
Live a life of liberty

Satan the blood is against you
And you cannot deny it
Not only will I live a victorious life now
But I'll never join you in the pit

WHEN I SEE HIS FACE

When I see His face, I'll know that I've finished my race
What a long, tedious journey it will have been
But throughout it all, I always knew I'd win

You may ask me, how do I know
Because the revealing word of God tells me so

Just to think, He and me
Standing face to face, to see
That all that He's promised, it's quite true
That it's not actually the time that I am through
It will just be the eternal beginning of a perpetual cycle
Of continuous winning

Right now, I know that when I'm in His presence
I experience warmth and a feeling that's most pleasant

He gives me faith that can no place else be found
He encourages me when there is no one else around

When I have a problem I can go to Him
Leave it with Him, obtaining a feeling of freedom within

But there's more

He has prepared a place for me
And one day that's exactly where I'll be

I see His face now within my mind
It's promising, luminous, stern and most kind

I feel Him now in a cool summer's breeze
Gently sweeping throughout the trees

I see Him now through countless deeds
Sent my way, providing my wants and needs

I see Him now again and again
Is there any wonder that I continue to win

I hear His enlightening voice
In the kindest of words
See His majesty as I observe this world
Right down to the most minute bird

I see His personage in the many people I meet
Here and there, or even, just walking down the street

Time and time again, His angels of mercy He sends
To watch over, guide, console me and then
Speak to me as friend to friend

He reveals to me, repeatedly, in so many ways
That we are living in the very last days

But oh! When I finally see His face
I'll certainly know that I've finished my race

What a long, tedious journey it will have been
But throughout it all, I always knew I'd win

The Giver

What is a true giver
He wanted to know

Is it someone who gives
Thinking that you reap what you sow

Is it someone who gives so
That he may be seen

Someone that gives, pursuing
An ambivalent dream

Is giving a mere act that
Suggests one is great

Or is it someone who
Calculates his givings to date

Perhaps it's that person
Who consequently thinks

Out of the fountain of
Retaliation will I drink

Could it be, would it be
Someone who
Believes that giving's just
The right thing to do

The man thought for awhile
And then something
Within him
Begin to reverberate these
Words of wisdom

It is someone who gives
So that others will live

Someone that experiences
An inner joy
Just by the very chance to give

A true giver is someone who
Gives out of the sincerity of his heart

And there isn't much that he has
That he would not be willing to part

I have seen people give and
Live life more abundantly
While others keep all
To themselves and end
Up quite redundantly

I don't have enough to give
I heard someone say
And that person is impoverished
To this very day

A true giver is someone
Who's willing to share

Someone who gives to
Show that he cares

He's that person who's
Willing to give his last

Not waiting for the chance
To give to pass

A true giver is
Willing to give his best

Not making excuses
Like some of the rest

Saying that they hoped
They had enough to give
A prosperous life they
Will not live

Look all around you
And try to see

Just what kind of giver
It pays to be

Who is a true giver
Now you know

It is someone that will
Cause themselves

And others, to grow

The Race

I'm at the starting line
And my mind's all in a flutter
Will I win this time
Or lose to another

I glance a sideways stare
At my opponent
Whose face is blank
I can beat her - I think

My mind is tumultuously
In a race of its own
Contemplating to give up
Renege, go home

But it's too late now
The bell has rung
Snapping me back to the reality
That the race has begun

We speed off together
Like galloping horses
Running, sweating, panting
As we're nearing our courses

The wind blowing on my face
Seems to whisper sweet victory
Losing, not winning, defeat
No! That's not what I see

Suddenly the finish line
Is in clear view
And I'm so happy about my
Potential win that I just
Don't know what to do

My opponent is slowing
Down now, how much
Better can this get
Nothing within my innermost
Being seems to suggest regret

The finish line is a few
Feet away now
There's no way that
I'm going to lose

But all of a sudden
My opponent finds
Energy that up until
Now, she hadn't used

As she zooms past
Me and the finish line
Like a bolt of lightning
From the sky
All my heart can do is
To say, Oh no! in a
Disparaging sigh

But believe it or not
She wasn't the only winner
I was a winner too

Because the next time
That I decide to run
A race, I'll know
What not to do

Stranger

A stranger crossed my path
Just the other day
And he straightway gained
My attention
As he began to say

I have been watching you
For a very long time
You seem to have so many
Disturbing things on your mind

Each day I observe you
Running here and there
And I've come to the
Conclusion that many
Hardships you bear

Your family that you love
So much add to your
Problems too
Because there is so much
Going on at home that
You don't know what to do

I listened intensely as he
Continued to say

I've heard that you take
Different medication all
Throughout the night
Hoping that they'll help
You to get some sleep
Hoping that they'll help
To make things all right

I have the answer for
All of your cares
Seek the Lord
While He might be found
Go to Him in prayer

Everything changed in
My life that day
I found the answer
I learned how to pray

The Master's Touch

The Master's touch is
Worth much more than gold
It goes beyond the physical mind
And heals the soul

His touch will cause an awakening
In our lives
Because for all of us he has
Paid a tremendous price

His touch will open up our eyes
And we'll receive blessings of
A proportional size

The Master's touch will make
Our dreams come true
It will turn our lives around and
We'll find enjoyment in all
We pursue

The master's touch will deliver us
From the yoke of bondage
And we'll witness many things in our
Lives turn around to our advantage

His touch will empower us to
Walk in victory
As we learn to not walk in our own
Ways but in those of
Divine integrity

His touch will enable us to
Live life more abundantly
As we from all sources of
Evil nature flee

His supernatural touch can
Heal the soul
And in every single area
Of our lives make us whole

No Distractions Allowed

You say how did he
Make it to the top

Why during his lifetime
Did he not become a flop

It's because he would
Not allow any distractions
To victimize him

He wouldn't allow
Circumstances to force
Him to live in sin

He put his eyes on the
Prize and would not
Turn around

That's why he's made
It to the top
And that his feet are
Planted on solid ground

When his buddies laughed
At him and tried to
Put him down

He continued to work
Towards a successful
Future and would not
Turn around

Someone tried to focus
His attention on using
Drugs

But he refused them
And told them that
He was strong willed
And didn't need a crutch

Another person told him
That he could be wealthy quick
That if he'd scheme to rob
People soon he'd be rich

No, I refuse to rob people
Was the answer that he gave
I am a devoted Christian
I am wholly saved

Because he pressed on and
Would not allow distractions
To hold him prey

He is still a victor
Right to this very day

It's a Mystery to Me

How can someone live without the Lord
It's a mystery to me
In Him we have our entire being
We breathe, we move, we see

How can one plan to spend the day
Without Him to clear the way
To protect, guide and fellowship
With them as they travel
Throughout the day

How can one expect to prosper
To be successful and feel free

How can someone live without the Lord
It's a mystery to me

A Wise Decision

I made a decision to say no to drugs
My parents helped me by giving
Me plenty of hugs

I made a decision not to live a low life
My teachers helped me by
Giving me good advice

Yes, I decided not to smoke cigarettes
My parents influenced me and
Now I have no regrets

I made a decision not to
Become an alcoholic
I steered my life into
Creative, worthwhile habits

Some of my friends said that
My life would be a drag
If I didn't develop some of the
Negative habits that they had

I chose to say no in spite of
Losing their so called friendship
I inclined my ears to
Every good spoken tip

They wasted their lives and for
Them many things went wrong

I'm grateful that I was wise enough
To be one that resisted pressure
And could stand on my own two feet

Now I go on and things are well with me
Because of the wise decision that
I made I live a life that's happy and free

Oh what the possibilities
Because I chose not to follow others
But just to be me

According to the word of God, what does Jesus have to say in our defense against the devil? What would Jesus say to him because He loves us so?

Lover's Quarrel

I created him in my image the Lord began to say
I know that it's because of this
That he'll serve and worship me every day

Oh no, you must be mistaken
I heard the devil say
Because he's ungrateful and selfish
He'll choose rather to walk in my ways

I've made him the head and not
The tail, God replied, to be
Above only
Given him abundance and a chance
To have a good heart, just like me

So what - the devil replied
I know this information too
And I'll do everything in my power
To see that he doesn't serve you

I've called him by name and
Sheltered and clothed him
I've revealed my promises to him
And let him know that in me he can
And will win

Oh yes, sure, I know that it's
Through you that he has
Been sheltered and fed

But it's through me on the other
Hand that, if I can have things
My way, he'll end up dead

No weapon that's formed against
My children will succeed
This I know that you know
It's in my unadulterated word
And whatever it says it's so

Be cast back into utter darkness
And leave my children alone
They're safe under the blood of Jesus
And as long as I sit on the throne

FAVOR

Is When.....

You're standing at the end of the line and
Suddenly you find yourself up front and
Wonder how you got there so fast

The judge sentences you to be put in
Jail and suddenly he changes his mind
And sets you free

You're given the best seat in the restaurant
Although it appears that it's crowded and
That there were many other people before you

You get a promotion on the job
Although someone else was there
Much longer than you

You get a surprise check in the mail

Someone sets a trap for you
And it turns out to be your biggest
Blessing

You've spent all of your money, or so
You think and then you find a one hundred
Dollar bill in your pocket

You go to sleep sick and wake up totally
Healed and feeling great

You go into a store and find a hidden
Treasure in the far corner behind other
Objects just waiting for your eyes only to
Uncover and purchase

Someone gives you a gift that you have
Desired for a long time

You go forth to battle a particular
Situation and God intervenes before
You can get there and all you have
To end up doing is put a smile on your face

You are given the gift of salvation
Although you could never have earned it

You are given hope in a world that
Is a picture of doom

Favor is when God watches out for you and
Pours out His blessings on you just because
He loves you

A Brand New Day

There was a young woman
Whose life had been shattered

She unfortunately was someone
That had been abused and battered

All of her life it seemed
That things had gone wrong
And she didn't even remember how to
Smile, it had been so very long

As she went through the ritual of
Getting up and going to work
She tried to hide the sad fact that
Her heart ached and her body hurt

She experienced such a lonely
Feeling of isolation
And had a feeling within herself
That there was no resolution

People would ask
Time and time again
Where are your relatives
Don't you have any friends

No, she would tell them with
Tears in her eyes
And the more that she
Thought about this
She felt very deprived

It seemed as if her life were
On a merry go round
And that any source of happiness

Could never be found
Then one day she met a new friend
And I can still hear him say
Come to church with me and with
That, for her, it began a new day

As soon as she walked
Through the doors she knew
That things never would
Again be the same
They'd be brand new

As she stood with uplifted
Hands during worship and praise
She began to feel peaceful and
Her spirit was raised

An empowering spirit began
To overtake her
And a feeling of unexplainable
Contentment began to occur

Her friend looked at her
With a smile on his face
I knew that if you came here
You'd get a blessing in this place

The minister began to preach the
Sermon and she was all ears
And she found out through his
Message that things for her were
Not as bad as they appeared

She received a new revelation
As she gave her heart to the
Lord that day

And all of her fears and
Anxieties vanished away

Now time has passed and
She's no longer alone
She's married to her friend
And they have a beautiful new home

Not only that but their beautiful
Children run around and play
Because of the commitment that
She made to the Lord that day

Spiritual Therapy

Close your eyes and bask in the
Promises of the Lord

That's spiritual therapy

Find a quiet place and read the Bible

That's spiritual therapy

Leaning on the Lord when your
Physical strength has diminished

Crying out to God in your time of need
And desperation

Fasting on a regular basis and
Focusing your mind on Jesus

That's spiritual therapy

Attending God's house of worship
Faithfully and anxiously anticipating
The move of the Lord

That's spiritual therapy

Asking God to give you knowledge and
Wisdom to handle all of life's circumstances

Yearning for a closer walk with God
And developing a partnership with Him

Resting in the words of the Lord and
Believing that each and every one
Of them is true

That's spiritual therapy

Having a closed ear to all that Satan
Has to whisper to you

Pursuing righteous living and having
Mercy on others

Reflecting on what God has done
For you, consequently developing
A spirit of gratitude

That's spiritual therapy,
An unfailing antidote against
The strongholds and problems
Of this world

Be Free!

Chains of captivity be broken
Be overpowered by the Holy Ghost portion
Powers of darkness disappear
For the spirit of the Lord is here

BE FREE!

Unsurrendering hearts yield
As the truth is revealed
Spirit of witchcraft cease
The power of the Holy Spirit increase

BE FREE!

Spirit of poverty be bound
Turning the lives of many,
Financially around
Financial blessings overtake
From the storehouse of the Lord radiate

BE FREE!

Spirit of drug addiction, alcoholism and
Desire to smoke cigarettes
In the name of Jesus Christ
We authorizingly reject

BE FREE!

Loneliness cease to be no more
As unto the Lord our heart's issues we pour
All roots of depression be outcasted
And the very cause of it through
Christ be unmasked

BE FREE!

Spirit of deception be imprisoned
As we experience a brand new vision
All of Satan's tactics be revealed
And the enlightening of the
Lord's purpose be sealed

BE FREE!

Tormented minds find peace
At the very sound of Christ's
Name being released
Hopeless attitudes disappear
As the victory in Jesus
Is made crystal clear

BE FREE!

Hidden voices be made silent
Replaced by those that
Aren't violent
God's voice be emphasized
So that it will be clearly recognized

BE FREE!

Angels go before us consistently
Protecting, guiding and leading

BE FREE!

Spirit of anxiety, strongholds
And fear
Let them all, miraculously, disappear
Disease and sickness be replaced
By the spirit of healing and
By God's grace

BE FREE!

Jesus died a long time ago
So that we may be free
So that even now, we can be free
Free from sickness, free to be prosperous, saved
And blessed in every area of our lives

In the name of Jesus Christ of Nazareth
BE FREE!   BE FREE!

The Anointing

The anointing breaks the yoke
and sets the captive free
I experienced this life changing
gift long ago
and it's the greatest thing that
could have ever happened to me

What is this energizing sensation sent
from above from day to day
It is the precious gift of God
that takes all of your cares away

The Holy Ghost will comfort you when
life's problems cause you to feel downcast
When you feel you have nowhere to turn
the Holy Ghost's power will last and last

We can activate the anointing in our lives
if we fast and pray
It will quicken our lives to avoid disappointments
and heal negative circumstances that we
face from day to day

It will open our eyes to God's blessings
And shower us with knowledge of peace and love
It will cause us to speculate Jesus'
coming back for us soon to join Him in
the heavens being lifted above

The Holy Ghost will help us to hold on when
our physical nature would give up
It will calm us down in riotous situations
and give us a continuous spirit of love

What is this supernatural transformation
operating in our lives from day to day

It is God's Holy Spirit, sent to us from above
to comfort us until Jesus comes back
to take us away

Stolen Treasure

You say that you got up this morning and
Did not have time to pray
No time to focus your mind on God's goodness
Before you started your busy day -

STOLEN TREASURE

You left the house without even saying
Thank you Lord for your daily provisions
You didn't even think twice
That He's the very cause of you living

STOLEN TREASURE

Throughout the entire day you pondered
On the thoughts of all the things that
You do not have or desire to pursue
Instead of joyfully, thinking about
The wealth of things that God has
So abundantly given to you

STOLEN TREASURE

Someone needed a helping hand
Or an encouraging word
You were too busy
So their faith wasn't stirred

STOLEN TREASURE

You arrived home
From work safely at the end of the day
But would you take time to
Praise God for that
No way!

STOLEN TREASURE

You fell asleep feeling you'd
Get up the next morning
No credit to the Lord
Not even a thought of Him

STOLEN TREASURE!

Wake up!
Don't allow Satan to continue
Stealing from you
Turn your face to the Lord
And put your hope in Him

Unshackled

You're free, he proclaimed
As I held out my hand

Never would I have to live
In bondage again

He whom the Son sets free
Is free indeed

These words ran through my mind

And suddenly a surge of peace
Circulated my entire being
That I alone could never find

I reflected back on the shackles
That had bound my feet and hands

I remembered how many times in my life,
I'd tried to get up, only to fall down again

You're free, he proclaimed again
Louder than before

A smile of enlightenment
Countenanced my face
And I walked out of the door

Beauty Is Only Skin Deep

Beauty is only skin deep
I heard someone say
And because I didn't conscientiously
Listen what a morbid price
I had to pay

All I could see was the shapely
Figure and curved body
The motion, the unmistakable
Sign language at that first party

The large, black eyes invited
Me to embark on a journey
To an ending that was dark

Come and visit me, her
Red lips solicited me
I can make you happier
Than you ever thought
You could be

I can cause you to experience
Things, that up until now
You've only experienced
In your dreams

Yes, she was beautiful
On the outside
Well cultured, well bred

But she passed on a fatal
Disease to me and
Now I'm dead

The Inheritance

They sat in a large room quietly
Anxiously waiting to hear
Their share of this grand estate
Hoping the time was very near

There were three of them that had come
To this massive place to see
All of the possessions left in the will
Just exactly what their share would be

Soon a tall man entering the room without hesitation
Observed their hopeful faces staring at Him in
anticipation

To the first one He turned and said loud and clear
There certainly is no reason for you to be here

All of your life you gambled, drank and smoked
Drove your vehicle all around town,
Even though your license was revoked

You lived a life that was selfish,
Full of envy, full of strife
You sought to be with many women,
Ran around consistently on your wife

Then, focusing His attention on the
Second person, He begin to say
You never tried to learn about me
Never desired to come to my place of worship,
The house of praise
Relentless and violently you spent many of your days
During your lifetime, you stole, deceived others and
complained
You consistently were a hypocrite

And even swore, using my name
You even considered murder
Yes! Even this thought was on your mind
You didn't spend much time doing many things that
were kind
You chose to do wrong instead of right and that's
Why you became spiritually blind
Your end, I must say, is dreary and bleak
Because for my source of direction and guidance
You chose not to seek

Then, turning to the last man that sat quietly, looking
at His face
A smile beamed from Him as He said, You're
definitely in the right place

To you I give the gift of life and I will tell you why
You accepted me into your heart one day and have
lived up
To the words, I'll serve you until I die

You had a will to serve me even through thick and
thin
You believed in my promises even when
Satan said you could not win

You listened not to those that told you to turn around
You stayed around strong willed Christians and
In my house you could always be found

When someone needed a helping hand they could
depend on you
You did all of these wonderful things just
As I expected for you to do

You sought wisdom and righteousness
And daily read my word

And because you depended on me wholeheartedly
Again and again your health was restored

Now prepare to be changed and live with me for
eternity

Now behold my glory and be.......just like me!

Thank You Lord

Thank you Lord for one more day
How you consistently take all of my sorrows away

I lift my voice to you in praise
For you faithfully abide with me all of my days

I close my eyes and think about
All of the problems that you've brought me out

I think about the way things could have been
If I hadn't listened to your voice
And continued to live in sin

I want to run and spin and shout
Because from all forms of darkness
You brought me out

Thank you Lord for all you've done
I am the appreciative, grateful one

I think about what you've done for me
How you sacrificed your only son

So many things run through my mind
Making me thankful all of the time

I'll not let any opportunity pass by me
To say thank you Lord

For you set me free

Friendship

I learned a lesson a long time ago
From a wise teacher, a treasure for me to know

A lesson about friendship and what it is really all about
One that is true, without a shadow of a doubt

A real friend is someone who observes your ways
So that he can be a strength to you all of your days

Someone that will be there when times get rough
One that can read between the lines
And will know when to be gentle and when to be tough

He will take up for you when others put you down
When all of your other so called friends
Are gone, he'll still be around

A real friend is someone that gives good advice
It is someone that speaks positive words over your life

Words of encouragement, worth more than gold
That will guide, fortress, and nurture the soul

A helping hand in the time of need
Is what a real friend will give

It's someone that will help you to see that it's
Worth living the life you live

Be sure to learn this most valuable lesson
A true friend is one's greatest possession

Life's circumstances sometimes prove to be bleak

And sooner or later, inevitably, some of
These will reach their highest peak

Along life's way be sure to seek
Your friends among the humble and the meek

The Hero Within You

There's a hero within you just waiting to be free
It's not listening to the voice of defeat that whispers, keep me
company

Whenever a challenge comes your way,
Don't let doubtful thoughts hold you prey

Release the faith that you've been given, so that
You can experience the very best of living

You could give in to the voice of defeat
But many things you could have had, you'll never reap

Great thoughts come and go, but many are a soft echo
You must act on them, perspectively, if you're ever going to grow

Yes! The golden ring is within your grasp
Although it may seem like a questionable task

Don't let this opportunity slip away
Don't give in to the procrastinating thought
Of, maybe some other day

Now is the time to adhere to the inner force
That was predestinated to be a guiding source

Now is the time to listen to your heart
And to think on sound principles taught to you
Of which you should never depart

Something from within you is bringing from the past
All of the experiences that are meant to last

Using the present to nurture and mold
Avoiding any negative things that could become a stronghold

Reaching into the future with the strong arm of destiny
Obtaining all the qualities and more than
You ever dreamed you could be

Yes! There's a hero within you just waiting to be free
It's not listening to the voice that whispers, keep me company

Release your God given nature and let it go free
Experience the best of life, the way that God planned for it to be

The Disguise

He stood before me very well disguised
With a seemingly reputable countenance
And thought provoking eyes

He was handsomely tall in statue
A quite pleasing sight to see
But there was something about him
That somewhat frightened me

He was dressed very stylish
Well attired in the color black
And the way that he stood
Gave me a feeling that he
Had majestic tack

But underneath it all I somehow knew
That if I listened to any thing he had
To say, I'd surely be through

He could, in no way, fool me
I began to realize
Because I looked at him illuminatingly
Through spiritual eyes

Eyes that revealed his true hidden nature
Ones that are given to warn one of danger

He stretched out his hand to me and
Gestured to follow after him

But my eyes revealed a veracious vision
That if I did my end would be grim

As he moved towards me with
An intentional stride

A voice declared to me from deep inside
Rebuke him immediately and
He will have to flee
Do it without hesitation and he
Could no longer bother me

As I spoke the words of rebuke
And shouted, "Leave me alone!"
The black, ominous shadow disappeared
And completely left my home

I'm grateful to have been given eyes
That make my pathways bright

Thank God for giving me spiritual eyes
To always protect me both day and night

The Road

He started out one bright, sunny day
Down the road of happiness, some might say

Plenty of money in his pockets
Speculative dreams in his head
Perceptual illusions to disguise the fact that he might have
something to dread

I'm leaving my problems behind, he thought
I can go far with the things I've been taught
I just know that I can do better without my family
No one to nag, depend on and harass me

I'm turning my back on my former life
Especially those burdensome children and that troublesome wife

Pushing these thoughts in his head aside, he stopped and looked up
at the sky
Oh! He thought. This is the kind of beauty that money could
never buy

With a quicker pace he walked down the road
Moving in a liberated nature, I've been told

After some time he came to an intersection leading into two
different directions

Looking both ways he tried to surmise the one
That would lead to happiness, peace, some fun

One road looked serene, green and peaceful
The other greener, more mysterious, more inviting
Stimulating to his eyes, spellbinding, more exciting

This is the road for me, he said
Turning to walk down the wrong one instead

For some time the sun shone brightly down upon him
The trees leaves whispered things that he wanted to hear
It seemed that even the animals that began to appear
Smiled at him - from ear to ear

How smooth and pleasant this road is, he thought
I always knew that happiness could not be bought

As time went on the air began to change
It smelled of an aromatic nature that was strange
A cold, weird wind began to blow
And frightening noises began to echo
Throughout the forest that this road had led the man to
He began to experience such discomfort that he did not know what
to do

I'm going to turn around and go back home
The man thought and never again will I roam

Then he began to walk back in the direction that he'd come from
Soon running, passing frightening trees and stepping on some
Branches that seemed to grab at his feet

And thorns that tore mercilessly at his flesh
I've got to get home! He cried, almost out of breath
As he continued to experience such pain as he never knew he could
He wished he were home - home, for good!

After several hours of continuous travel
Over branches, huge rocks, boulders and gravel
The man saw his house in the distance
And for a while he just stood there, eyeing it as if he were in a
trance
Then, pulling himself together, he began to advance

When he finally reached home, he breathed a sigh of relief
Realizing that being there was more valuable than anything he'd
ever sought
As he knocked on the door and waited, once again, but in a
different way he thought
I always knew that happiness could not be bought

But when he turned the doorknob and proceeded to walk inside
Every hope and matrimonial dream in his head died

One look around the empty home and he most certainly knew
That he wasn't the only one who'd decided to leave

His family had left too!

Everlasting Fire

There's an everlasting fire and it's burning in my soul
But I know it won't engulf me, even though
It's brighter than any flame that I could ever behold

When I would be cold and desolate
And focus on circumstances that could cause regret

This burning fire is ignited and more warmth and comfort flows
From it than I could ever, physically, get

Piercing any situation of darkness, overpowering the night
Filling my entire being with complete and uncomprehending delight

It's an inextinguishable fire that burns on and on
Totally keeping me focused, continuously making me strong

All of my heartaches and miseries have passed
It gives me power to overcome and last

This everlasting fire will always tend to be
A supernatural source of strength and victory for me

I'm Washed In The Blood of the Lamb

They wonder why I don't do those things
Gossip, murmur, backstab and complain
It's because pleasing God is my aim,
For I'm washed in the blood of the Lamb

Why doesn't she covet and steal, they say
Seek earthly treasures to have things her way
I'd rather fast, help others and pray,
For I'm washed in the blood of the Lamb

What is her problem they sometimes think
Why doesn't she do drugs, smoke or drink
It's because with the Lord's ways
These things don't link
For I'm washed in the blood of the Lamb

Will she party the night away
Some of God's commandments disobey
I can, assuringly, answer, nay
For I'm washed in the blood of the Lamb

Each day I strive to do my best
Although sometimes ere, I must confess
Onwards, towards heaven I'll persistently press
For I'm washed in the blood of the Lamb

What Is Your Purpose In Life

Think about this question
Can you answer it in your mind
Will you stop for a moment
And for your destiny make some time

What is your purpose in life

What is on your mind when
You get up each day
Is it to live a most meaningful life
As you go on your way

Do you pre-plan to encourage
Others when they're downcast
Is your conversation to them
One that will help them to last

When you look into the real mirror
Of life that reflects the inner you
Do you feel satisfaction
Through and through

Are your thoughts positive ones
That will overpower any evil tool
Ones that will help you
To conquer and to rule

Do you rehearse in your mind
To find time each day
To put aside trivial discrepancies
That could hold you prey

Do you depend on the Lord
To control your every step
To divinely lead and guide you
As you seek him stedfastly in prayer

Is your presence one that
You think is coincidental
That you have no say in it
In no way is it intentional

The Bible says that the Lord
Has called you by name
And that you were predestinated
To depend on Him and reign

That you should call on Him
And open your ears to His will
And that if you do this
He'll with his spirit your life fill

That if you live a lifestyle
That is pleasing unto Him
That He'll fellowship with you
Consistently, again and again

You were predestined to worship
Him and praise Him daily
These actions were planned
A long time ago so that we can live
A life that's free

If you meditate on Jesus He'll show you
your true purpose in life

And consistently all of you needs and
desires he'll provide

Great Expectations, The Sermon

I'm expecting great things of the Lord, I can still hear him say
Through low or high waters, good and bad times, come what may

As the audience listened intensely he continued to say

Yes, look to the Lord and He'll dry all of your tears away
That's why we can have great expectations on this day

Learn to be stedfast in His word, learn to fast, learn to pray
Enter the Lord's house with a praise on your lips
And the Lord will see to it that your foot never slips

We need to be witnesses for the Lord as never before
To tear down every stronghold and to knock on every door

If we truly expect to get God's best, we've got to shake off
Disappointments, poverty and regret

As His words continued to reverberate throughout the great temple
Many minds and hearts were changed, a task that definitely was
not simple

We've got to seek the Lord daily from morning to night
And to not give in when satan attacks, but render a perseverant fight

We must have a new vision, one that supersedes the old
One that can use the past, only to nurture and to mold

A vision that facilitates those that are in need, that unselfishly denies
oneself to see that others may receive

A vision that reaches out with the strong arm of spiritual destiny
fulfilling
the gospel and setting people free

We must pay our tithes and offering, too
Because of God's goodness, this is one of the least things that we can
do
As is said in the word of God, do so and yes, God said prove

Me if I will not open up the windows of heaven and pour out a
blessing
you will not have room enough to receive
One that will cause you to spiritually, mentally, physically and
financially
achieve
Walking to the other side of the platform he went on to impart

Don't forget to be grateful for the big things, for the small ones too
And even greater things will God abundantly do for you

Have a song in your heart and keep your mind on Him
And the Lord will prove to be your very best friend

We can expect for angels to be all around us throughout the day
Going before us opening and closing doors, protecting, consoling and
guiding our way

We will flourish and succeed at this time, he continued to go on and
it's
because our faith is grounded in the Lord that blessings and miracles
will
not be prolonged

We're not in the valley but on the mountain standing as high as we
can be
And I know that God's best will continue to overtake you and me

Oh yes, I have great expectations, right now, on this very day

We have great, great expectations
Because our Lord, Jehova Jireh, is leading the way

Blood Issue

Long ago a woman had
Searched so very near and far

She had an issue of blood
It has been told
And all of her possessions
She had sold

She had tried so desperately
To get well, to be set free
Of all her pain and misery

She had seen many doctors
From day to day
Hoping that they could
Take her pain and suffering away

Then one day she heard
That Jesus was coming to town
And began to believe that she could
Be set free - no longer bound

This woman began to strategize in her mind
How that she could prepare a way
So that Jesus she could find

Her faith began to help
Her to get to Him

As she pushed her way
Through the crowd
Holding her back she would not allow

Finally, she touched the hem of His
Garment that day
And, instantly, all of her pain
And suffering went away

There's a most valuable lesson
In this biblical story for us
We can be set free from
Any of our diseases
If in God we will put our trust

Heart's Song

Lord, let me always have a grateful heart
For when I'm thanking you for things
You've done for me and the many situations
That you've brought me through

I'm reminding myself of your greatness
And that nothing is impossible for you
I'm reminding myself that you will take
Care of me in the future, no matter what

I'm reminding myself that my life is filled
With your blessings and not just sheer luck
I'm reflecting in my mind that you are the very
Reason that I can see, hear, feel, think and
Even breathe right now
And that without you there is nothing that
I can do, no way - no how!

I am focusing my attention on you because I
realize that you are the answer to all of my problems
All of my heartaches, illnesses and headaches,
Only you can supernaturally solve them

I have found so many ways to say thank you
That the list goes on and on
I will mention a few to you now
So dear Lord, Listen to my heart's song

Thank you for allowing me to rise day by day
To open my eyes every morning and
Prepare myself to start on my way

Even in a world that is full of confusion
You consistently give me peace of mind
And eyes that can see the truth
So that I will not be spiritually blind

I lift my hands up high to you
As a sign of my love and complete surrendering
It's just another way for me to
Show that I'll always love and worship you

If I had a thousand tongues I could go on and on
But this still wouldn't be adequate enough
To sing to you all of my - heart songs

Safe in the Word of the Lord

I trust in the Lord with all of my might
For He's my protector both day and night

When others shake their heads
And throw up their hands
I look to the hills from whence cometh my help and
Because of this I can stand

He promised to forever be by my side
Through heartaches and problems
Never forsaking to be my guide

Why don't I worry`
You might want to know
It's because I'm safe in the word of the Lord
Reaping what I sow

He's told me in His word that He'd open every door
To shelter, clothe and feed me, and even more
That the riches of this world and heaven are mine
What better treasures could
Anyone ever hope to find

Blessings going out and coming in I heard the Lord say
Victory over every situation and new mercies every day

Why don't I worry

Now you know

I'm safe in the word of the Lord

Just Me

In all the world, there'll never be
Another person exactly like me

I knew in my heart, right from the start
That my unique personality
Would be my most precious reward

My face, it's me
My hands, they're me
My mind, all of my features
They're me, just me

I'm a star that is shining bright
For all to see
To love, to nurture, to mold, to be
The very best that I could ever be

I have such potentiality
Because I'm free - just to be me

Insight

Open up my eyes Lord that I may see
All of the negative strategies that satan plans for me
Let me put on your whole armor so
I can be protected against principalities wherever I go

Let not abrupt situations cause me to do
Anything at all that does not exalt you
Help me to see beyond my physical eyes
Work in me to be perfect, healthy and wise

Give me the insight to those things usually hidden
Leave all areas of my life in your hands that need revision
Let me consistently focus my attention on you
So that I can have peace of mind my whole life through

Let me become a consistent reader of your
Word so that I can obtain enlightening understanding
Because life's circumstances are
Sometimes quite demanding

I will meditate on your word both day and night
I know that it's the key to help me to do right
Let there be a compassionate yearning in my soul
That will allow you to handle any situation
That may seem to be out of my control

I realize that I'll need to live a circumspective life
And can if I make my body a living sacrifice
I know that this physical body sometimes gets weak
But Lord I thank you for giving me a desire to seek
Those things that are pleasing unto you

Yes! You've assuringly shown me
That you're my closest friend too
I'm so blessed to be able to see
All that you have promised and the wonderful
Things that you so abundantly have planned for me

Fellowship

I hear you calling out to me in so many different ways
In a voice so loud and clear that it cannot be ignored
Come and fellowship with me it cries
As the thunder echoes on a stormy night

Put everything else aside
and focus your attention on me
You feel your schedule is hectic
And there's so much that you need to do

You feel there isn't a vacant spot on your calendar

Stop and focus your attention on me
I need to fellowship with you
Have you forgotten that I created you
for the sole purpose of worshipping me

Sometimes you feel lonely, unsatisfied, dismal and even ill
It's because you have forsaken to make time to fellowship with me
Always remember that I am your strength, your peace
The very air that you breathe

I am the very essence of your existence, your life, your destiny
I long to see your face anxiously looking to me
To hear your voice calling out to me, reverencing me,
Acknowledging me, praising me, exalting me

Never forsake to make time for me
For I am your God and I long to fellowship with you

PURSUIT

He searched for peace in riches, but it could not be found
Vainlessly achieving financial success,
Still going in circles, around and around

He searched for it in his talents, displaying
His abilities for all to see
Still, not even his best performance
Could help him obtain his dream to be free

He searched for it in alcohol and all kinds of drugs
Cigarettes, ill affections and artificial hugs

He searched for peace in religion
Believing that at last he had found the key
But soon learned you can't just follow
Tradition and really succeed at being free

Finally, just when it seemed to him
That all hope was gone
Someone came along and told him about Jesus
How he could turn his life into a happy song

Now his search has ended
And a jubilant expedition has begun

Because he found what he needed all of the time

Jesus Christ, God's precious Son

PITCH BLACK

Hanging out with your old home boys
Following after so called worldly joys

Partying until the brink of dawn
Deceivingly thinking, it can do me no harm

PITCH BLACK

Walking in your own covetous ways
Planning a life style you should evade
On and on until your end of days

PITCH BLACK

Focusing on a loose way of life
Not willing to listen to spiritual advice
Closing your eyes to the words of truth
Rather ominous ventures you choose to pursue

PITCH BLACK

The wages of sin is death, that's for sure
And by not obeying God you will endure
The end of a shallow grave that won't be secure

PITCH BLACK

Visions of the Sunset

Have you ever watched the sunset
What a beautiful display of nature
Streams of color bursting forth on everything,
Green, yellow, blue, orange and purple
Losing its vividness
As the sunsets

Once an array of streamers casting
Bright shadows against houses, mountains,
And valleys and then dark shadows
As the sunsets

Reflections in the waters, brilliantly contrasting
Getting fainter, becoming darker
Echoes of the end of another day
Darkness encaptivates the earth
As the sunsets

Where did the day go, I reminisce
As the sunsets and
What will tomorrow bring

Whatever, whatever
I'm safe in the Lord's hands

Just When

Just when you think there will be no tomorrow
Someone comes along and relieves all of your sorrows

Just when you thought you were a defeated loser
You come to realize that, not others, but you
Are your worst accuser

Just when you yearned to give up forever
Circumstances change and you achieve
Your dreams and every endeavor

Just when it seemed as if darkness were your best friend
Something took place in your life that
Lets you know, yes, you can win

Just when, just when, just when

If you hold on, you can win, you can win

He Alone

He alone can cause the day to turn to night
He can cause the calmness of waters
Or make them a raging, terrible sight

With a quiet whisper of his voice
He can take all pain away
With a touch of His hand
Illness miraculously disappears, without delay

Can't you see Him standing,
With outstretched hands to you
Promising a lifetime of commitment
To love and to carry you through

Can't you feel Him waiting for you to knock on the door
Turning from all of your sorrows, gaining
Earthly inheritances and even more

Be prepared to stand before Him
One day face to face
Realizing that through it all
You've victoriously finished the race

Sleep In Heavenly Peace

I can sleep peacefully
because someone is always watching over me

Nothing can challenge or torment my mind
I experience the best relaxation that one could ever find

I don't have to worry about bills being paid
Because everything on the earth my God has made

Pain and suffering sometimes keep one awake
Or things that could happen that they might anticipate

Feelings of anxiety sometimes try to impede
But depending on the Lord will cause them to leave

One might think that I should worry because
Sometimes circumstances look brink

No! The master is watching over me
And all I have to do is on His word to think

I could focus my attention on catastrophes all around
Or on many other negative things that usually get people down

But I know that God can solve anything and everything
And it's because of his overpowering nature
That my heart can still sing

I will continue to sleep, sleep in heavenly peace
Because God is always watching over me

Testimony

I have a testimony that I'd like for all to know
God has been a refuge and strength
And throughout my life was faithful to show
To me the road to happiness and also peace of mind
Far beyond the so called success of this world
No other such place of refuge could I find

Out of darkness he brought me into the marvelous light
Caused me to realize that the real secret
Of success is in doing what's right

Caring for the poor, adhering to their needs
Lending a helping hand to others
Always positively sowing seeds

Releasing the power within me to individuals all around
Trying to minister to all kind of needs so that
They can survive and their minds be sound

Leaning on the mighty arms of Jesus
Listening to His encouraging words

Looking to Him to brighten my pathways
Knowing that His truth is sharper than
Any two-edged sword

Remembering how He mercifully saved me
From a world of sin and shame
Thinking about how He made me a new creature
And in the book of life has written my name

I have a testimony that I'd like for all to know
And I know I'll keep on telling it
Everywhere I go

Fruit of Your Ways

As we go about our business
Hurrying around from day to day
What kind of fruit are we producing
As we travel along life's highway

Does our fruit create a sweet fragrance
Rising up into the nostrils of the Lord
Or is it a stench that develops
From our sinful nature and a corrupt heart

Do we operate in the spirit
And produce fruit that is sweet and pure
Choosing good over evil decisions
So that our lives will meaningfully endure

Does our presence around others
Produce an environment of peace
Or is persecution, stress and animosity
The fruit that we release

Do showers of blessings follow us
As we move around
And we consistently speak positive words to
Others in an effort that their minds be sound

Just what kind of fruit
Are we producing each day
Is it the kind that would cause
Someone's sorrows to go away

Does our fruit speak of thankfulness
Through the lives that we lead
A condition that sticks with us
Because we realize we've been set free

What kind of fruit are we indeed
Producing as we go along the way
Think about this question
As you live from day to day

I Am the Best
(Original Version)

I am the best! Yes! I am the best!
I pass each and every single test.
Because I concentrate on winning and I usually do,
I mediate on good things and that's best for you.
You know, an educated mind just can't be beat,
When it's full of knowledge, you have limited defeat.
What! What! Don't you know that it's time to wake up?
The winners are the ones that are all booked up.
That's why I get to school early so I won't lose time,
You see, I'm working very hard to educate my mind.
Education is gain is my philosophy. It's one major
Thing you have to set yourself free.
Man can take some things away from you, but with your
Confidence and knowledge there is nothing he can do.

I am the best! Yes! I am the best!
I pass each and every single test!

I Am the Best

A young woman picked up her pen one day
and she began to write. She had a feeling that
her next poem would shatter the darkness and
reveal light. These are the words that she wrote
down that day, and if you have a listening ear I
believe they will show you the way:

I am the best!
Yes! I am the best!
I pass each and every, single test

Because I concentrate on winning
And I usually do
I mediate on good things
And that's best for you

You know a consecrated life
Just can't be beat
When it's filled with prayer
You have limited defeat

What! What! Don't you
Know that it's time to wake up
The winners are the ones
That are all prayed up

That's why I steer my life towards
Worthwhile ventures everyday
I invite Christ to share it
So that He'll show me the way

I read the word of God consistently
So that I can develop His
Character and live a life that's free

I am the best!
Yes! I am the best!

I pass each and every, single test!

Masterpiece

With His own hands He created
This world with its dry land and many seas

Yes, He also created the fish in the sea

Each and every master-piece

He changed darkness into light
And also created the day and night
Nothing is here now that God's
Voice didn't release

Each and every master-piece

He made the sun
So bright and great
And placed it up high
So that we could escape
Its powerful, streaming
Outreached hands

But even these the Lord commands

He made the moon
We know for sure
And throughout the night
Its light endures
Illuminating the night and so
In complete darkness
We don't have to go

He created the animals big and small
The bear, deer, whale and all
The birds that fly around in the sky
He created them all, even you and I

More than our minds can imagine
Much more than we can see
God is the one
That created it all

Each and every master-piece

A Daily Recipe For Success

Get up in the morning
With a grateful heart

Praise God for all of His blessings
Right from the start

Sing praises of His goodness
Even as you pray
Thank Him in advance
For a successful day

Throughout the day sing
Spiritual melodies in your heart
And God's faithfulness
To lead and guide you
Shall be your reward

Think on the scriptures
All throughout the day
It's a definite measure
To take all of your anxieties away

Bless the Lord at all times
I've heard the scriptures say
His praise shall continually
Be in my mouth
Day after day after day

Reach out to others with a
Helping hand
Forsake worldly pleasures
And on God's word stand

Plan to make time for Him
To read His word and pray
This is a scriptural recipe
That will keep satan's
Tactics away

Don't forget to delight
Yourself in Him
So that the desires of your
Heart will be ushered in

There are many recipes for success
In the world today

But none of them can cause
Total success and take all pain away

Always remember and don't forget
God's recipe for success is the best one yet.

You Put a Smile On My Face

Jesus, You put a smile on my face
When I think about all that
You've done for me

When I feel your presence
Consistently running through
And exhilarating me

It's surely not hard to explain
Why there's so much power in your name

I want to focus my attention on you
And acknowledge your guidance
In everything that I do

When I'm feeling Lonely
Downcast or depressed
You speak to me gently
And cause my mind to be at rest

My heart experiences
Such joy in you
Because in every situation
You've proven yourself
To be true

Jesus, I will worship
You all of my days
Because you consistently
Put a smile on my face

In The Presence of the King

In the presence of the King the blind
Eyes open and one can see

The crippled stand up and walk, supernaturally

Yes! In His presence the deaf and dumb speak
And for His majestic attention we humbly seek

In the presence of the King
There is rest for the weary soul
And if you have the spirit of fear
God's power will overtake it and make you bold

In the presence of the King we get
More strength to run this race
And we experience great power just by looking at His face

Those that have lost hope
Find it in the presence of the King
He gives them a new vision in life
And a new song to sing

It is in His presence that we are justified
That our eyes are really opened to
The fact of just why Christ died

In His presence the dead are restored
To life and can breathe again
They're empowered to make up their minds
That they will never again live in sin

We experience such joy and peace untold
As God speaks to us and His mysteries unfold

Oh, for the opportunity to be
In the presence of the King
It brings you more deliverance than
Anything on earth could ever bring

It makes you want to laugh and run
Jump and sing

Oh! Let me live my life consistently
In the presence of the Holy King!

The Secret Place

The secret place of the most high
That's where I want to be
For it's in this royal habitation
That my entire being experiences liberty

Chains of bondage are broken
In the presence of the Lord
Peace, healing and joy overtake
Me as we, He and I come to one accord

It is the secret place of the most
High that all evil inspiration die
And we become spiritually rejuvenated
As to the Lord we draw nigh

In the secret place we can
Go humbly to the Lord
And tell Him everything
Not one secret must we avoid

Now receive a revelation
That I've heard loud and clear
The secret place isn't really secret
Because the Lord, Jesus Christ, is right here

Rescued

He almost died in a black, raging sea of death
But the Lord rescued him and took him into His rest
It happened not so very long ago
When his life was upside down
And looked as if it would end in a state of woe

I, for one, witnessed this happening to him
What a horrible sight to see
As he was lifted by a terrible black shadow
And thrown into the midst of the sea

I never will forget the terror
That I felt within my heart
When I witnessed this nightmare unfolding
Right from the terrible start

Someone dived in after Him
Although the waters were murky and dark

Someone told him about Jesus and that
He should not delay in giving Him his heart

All of a sudden he was standing on
A dry foundation - land
He cried and jumped up and down
So relieved to be saved and a changed man

Now he is elevated for everyone to see
And I am praising God in my heart
Because that someone that helped him is me

Not Today

He stumbled out of bed
In a state of confusion
And looked around disoriented
As if he'd seen an illusion

He slowly turned his head to see that
The television was still playing
And faintly he could hear
The words that the minister
Was saying

Today is your day
Don't let it pass
Promise that you'll
Give your heart to
The Lord, at last

Don't wait another minute
Don't continue to live in sin
Say that you'll accept
Him into your heart
So that you'll be born again

He's stretching out His hand to you
Trying to convince you
Attempting to rescue you
From this world of sin and shame
So that with Him you can reign

Won't you let Jesus come
Into your life
Won't you take
My spiritual advice

Not today

The man said as he
Walked into the bathroom
Then he thought about the fact
That he had to get to work soon

He washed up and ate
In fact, cleaned his plate

He got dressed and left
Starting down the steps

But before he knew it, he
Was tumbling down
Over and over, around
And around

When he got to the bottom
There he lay
And he couldn't get up
So he had to stay

By the time the ambulance
Got there it was too late
The young man had suffered
A terrible fate

When I read this story I
Learned an important lesson too

When God calls for you to follow Him
Make sure that you do

Criminal

He sat in the jail cell with a
reminiscent look on his face
Past hardships, tragedies and
criminal activities on his countenance
could be traced

He reflected back to the time when he
was a little boy
How he'd had a wonderful childhood
full of happiness and joy

Someone changed the picture
Something began to speak to his mind
and evil thoughts he began to employ

He started listening to voices
of the wrong kind
Voices that stole his dreams
and gave him a wicked mind

Walk in our ways and you'll be free
they lied to him from day to day

Don't forget to listen to us
and never, ever try to pray
Reading the Bible is out
that's for sure
If you decide to read that book
under our power you cannot endure

Close your eyes to the truth
for that's only for fools
You need our sovereign devices
as your most valuable tools

As he began to see the whole
picture of his life in his mind
Someone walked into the cell and
touched him and he began to experience
a revelation of a supernatural kind

He decided in his mind to change that day
He got up from the bed and began to pray

As the tears of deliverance
ran streaming down his cheeks
He felt the powerful, life changing
spirit of love
He felt complete victory

Lord thank you for opening
up my eyes that I might see

Thank you for giving me the victory

Never again will I suffer from a
criminal mind

I'm going to be the best saint
that you could ever find

Twice Blinded

The young man had beautiful, long hair
running down his back
but a beautiful, young woman
cut it off, as a matter of fact

After that he wasn't very strong at all
That's when he suffered his devastating fall

How could this have happened
he wanted to know
It's because as the good book
says, you reap what you sow

He had closed his eyes in the lap
of a beautiful woman who had
spoken enticing words
Words used to trick him,
encaptivating cords

Then when he shook himself
as he'd done so many times before
he found out that he didn't have
his supernatural strength anymore

His enemies moved in on him as
quickly as they could
chained, tortured and blinded him
as they had planned they would

When he felt that all hope was gone
Jesus supernaturally came along

He gave him his strength back
just for a little while
so that he could pull the
temple down

Although this is an unfortunate
way for things to be
He still got what he wanted
in his state of desperation
to be free

"Don't turn your back on the devil, rather,
be children of the light."

Forgive

Forgive, so that you may live
The teacher began to say

Turn your back on the spirit of
Unforgiving so that
Your life, it won't delay

Oh, someone did something to you
That you feel is unforgivable
Something so terrible that you
Feel through the pain it's
Unlivable

But who do we hurt most often
When we hold these feelings in
Who is the one that suffers
Heartaches again and again

It is us the ones who
Decide to never give in
By us continuing to be this way
We simply just can't win

One woman said she forgave
Her sister today
And that instantly her much
Long suffered headache went away

A young man said he'd forgiven
His mom and dad too
And that he was experiencing so much
Joy that he just didn't know
What to do

Still another person smiled at me
And began to say
When I forgave my children a terrible
Disease that I had went away

Yes, just think about it
Could it really be true
Can you experience so much
Happiness if forgiving ways you pursue

Forgive - so that you and others may live

Train Up a Child

Train up a child in the way he should go
And he won't depart from it
The Bible says so

When he is old enough to
Make choices in life
That's the time to begin
Giving him good advice

Take time to talk to
Him again and again
Teach him Godly principles
So that he won't live in sin

Yes, be sure to teach him right
From wrong so that when he grows
Up he will be healthy and strong

Trained children are a pleasure to be around
They develop positive manners and
A mind that is pleasing and sound

Trained children are a joy to their
Relatives and friends
For where training ends
Wisdom begins

A trained child will experience
Many positive things in life
He'll treasure sound doctrine
And accept Godly advice

Train up a child in
The way that he should go
And when he grows old
He won't depart from it

The Bible says so

He Sets A Table Before Me

He sets a table before me
With delicacies beyond compare

A measure of good health
A pinch of spice
And a peaceful life
With the help of prayer

The best food He prepares for me
A most majestic, delicious feast
Satisfying my hunger and giving
Me more than I could ever
Desire or need

Oh taste and see that
The Lord is good
These words run
Through my mind
As I sit at this beautiful table
Time after time after time

Each day I know
I'll be served the best
Because I've learned to
Safely in God's word rest

Each day I know I'll
Be satisfied
Because in my life
By His word I'll abide

To worry about any
Source of starvation
I know I never will

Because I fully trust
In Jesus and my
Life has been sealed

Revelation

The Lord will open
Your eyes to the truth
To guide you in every situation
He'll carry you through

Revealing life's potential woes
He'll whisper to your life
Golden truths

A comforting voice to lead you
To help you pursue life's best
Summoning you to live His word
So that you'll be empowered
To pass any test

Quietly but firmly releasing
Hidden truths as you
Demonstrate your faithfulness
In everything that you do

The Lord will open
Your eyes to the truth
To guide you through
Every situation that
You go through

Chosen Generation

There's a chosen generation
The young man began to proclaim
God has called a peculiar people
And one day He'll call us all by name

A people who will stand for right
When other choose to do wrong
A people that live by the word of God
And in their hearts have a devoted song

Focusing their eyes on God
In every situation
Showing all that they obey Him
That they're a loyal nation

We are a royal priesthood
The young man went on to say
And our determination to serve the
Lord is tested everyday

It is not easy to be loyal subjects
In everything that we do
To walk just right
To also talk right
And always remain true

But it helps us because we
Remember that God has
Paid a tremendous price

When He sent His son Jesus
To die on the cross
Encaptivating the darkness
Releasing the light

We will continue to serve Him
Because He is our King

He is our shepherd, deliverer,
Friend and doctor

Yes, He is our everything!

All Hail King Jesus

All hail King Jesus
Who sits upon the throne
Who was created long, long ago
Even before the earth was formed

What a mystery to think that
He walked here in the flesh long
Ago just as we do today

Yet he yielded not to temptation
And did miracles everywhere
His life was dedicated as a
Living sacrifice so that we might
Have a right to the tree of life

Just to think that even while
Man was yet in sin Jesus
Christ died for us all!
So that ultimately we would win

What an unusual servant

What a majestic king

All Hail King Jesus!

Wisdom

The gift of wisdom is priceless
The visitor began to say

It will protect and extend your
Life as you experience it each day

It will remind you of the past
And how you've gained experience

It will speak to you in the present
And help you to be firmly grounded

Wisdom will pave a path
With it's enduring light

It will shine a light of intuition
And understanding before
You and make your
Pathways bright

Wisdom will open many doors
That would otherwise be
Closed instead

It will give you the insight to
Realize that because you're
In Christ you have
Nothing at all, to dread

He who searches for
Wisdom will find it
The Bible says

He will feast on it day and
Night and be overwhelmingly fed

You Belong To Me

You belong to me
That's why I created you in liberty
Out of the innermost parts
Of my majesty I longed to
Fellowship with you and
Share my destiny

To be able to call you by name

To be able to call you my own
So that you never would have
To walk in darkness or be alone

To be able to hear your voice
And to know even before you were born
That you'd make the right choice

I created you in spirit and in truth
So that you could be a celebration
Of life and acknowledge me
In all that you do

You belong to me

I created you to praise my name
And if you stedfastly do my will
Of you, I'll never be ashamed

You are my daughter, my son
I am your Father, the holy one

You belong to me

And that is why I love you so
I want you to live in victory
More than you'll ever know

You belong to me

And one day you will see
That I made you to live with
Me for all eternity

The Answer

What is the answer for the world today

Who is all powerful and can take
All troubles away

Who is the one that is concerned about
Our welfare

One who will listen and always be there

Christ is the one who will heal our
Sinsick soul

Who will also give us far more than
Silver and gold

He healed many and walked on the sea

Surely, I know that He's the answer
For you and me

Salvation

Seeking
    Believing
        Repenting
            Meditating
                Changing
                    Saved

Witnessing

Prepared to go to heaven with Christ
When He returns!

Encourage Yourself

Encourage yourself
Don't let yourself down
For you are still there
When no one else is around

Speak positive words over your life
Forsake verbal put downs
Self anger and strife

Encourage yourself to do good
And not wrong
Sing yourself happy
With an uplifting song

Treat yourself special
And reward yourself too
Because there's no one else
In the world like you

You're a unique individual
Framed after the Lord
And if you live according
To his will
You'll receive a heavenly reward

True Gifts

True gifts are sincere smiles
Given by others who daily pass our way

They are sweet smelling flowers
Spreading in splendor on a sun shiny day
They are so fragrant that it
Gives new life to you
Initiating an appreciation for living
And generating a feeling of rebirth too

True gifts are kind acts of praise
Echoing in your ears
A hug of affection, an appreciated tear
Someone standing beside you
Year after year

A sweet song resounding to the
Depths of your soul is another
Of life's cherished treasures
The feeling of warmth and joy
That it inspires can never, ever
Be measured

True gifts are eyes that sparkle
Brighter when they're
Looking at you

Ears that listen patiently and
Yearn to hear you too

True gifts are people that are
Willing to lend a helping hand

Whenever everything is falling
Around them, God will
Enable them to stand

The best gift of all is the
Gift of love
And each and every one of
These gifts is sent from God above

Bountiful Blessings

Bountiful blessings
Sent from above

A clear expression of an
Unconditional love

Daily benefits
The best to be found
Transforming my mind
And turning my life around

Spiritual blessings
And physical too
Sent from the Lord and more
Than enough to prove

He loves me so and will
Be here always
To carry me through
For the rest of my days

Bountiful blessings
Sent from above
A clear, clear expression
Of an unconditional love!

Echoes Throughout The Day

There are echoes in my soul
Resounding throughout the day

Cleaning me, filling me
Taking all of my sorrows away

Sing Hosanna, Jubilant praise
Thinking and singing and
Walking in His ways

Echoes that bombard my
Mind throughout
Keeping out all anxiety and doubt

Sing Hosanna, Jubilant praise

I'm going home one of these days

Mention

Dear God,
You promised that your ears would be open to my prayers
That if I created an atmosphere of praise that you'd be there

I'm taking this time to mention your word
Because I know it will not return unto me void

I believe in my heart that if I keep it on my mind
That I'll receive many a reward

I'm mentioning how you've said that
You would have me to prosper,
Be in good health and experience great joy

How that your word says that if I walk
In your ways and obey your commandments
That's the best choice

You said to remind you about all of
The promises that you have spoken to me about

That you'd perform many miracles in my
Life if I believe on your word, without a doubt

I know that thou art ready to forgive and
Are plentiful in mercy to all that call upon thee

I make mention that you've said you'd
Help me so that I would not be
Confounded, but rather quite free

Lord in your word, it says that you
Daily load me with benefits and
This is so true

For without your many sources of meeting
My daily needs, what would I do

Be reminiscent Lord of the peace that
Surpasseth all understanding that you've
Promised would be given to me
If I keep my mind on you and
Sincerely worship thee

I make mention of your word and in
My heart it will stay
So that I can have faith and victory
Because of it each and every day

Conquest

You're going to lose, the giant bellowed
As she stood before him in full armor

She knew by the giant's hopeful threats
That he'd do anything to harm her

Even the weather thundered and
Lightning flashed in the sky

Seemingly to agree with the giant
Oh yes! You're going to die

A tear rolled down her cheek
because of the fear that was in her heart

As she stood before this huge monstrosity
A petrifying picture
that was dreary and dark

Faintly, but strongly, a voice from
within began to echo these words of old

He comes to steal, kill and destroy
Was revealed in the Bible
since long ago

She began to recall many stories
That she'd been taught by
Her parents and teachers

That when you accept
Christ into your life, you become
A victorious, new creature

How God had brought His people
Out of Egypt, even though
Pharaoh fought, venomously
not to let them go

That God sends angels to
protect us when we are in need

How He allowed Jesus to be born
And then, sacrificed His only seed

These recollections
bombarded her mind

Of God's miraculous intervention
Again and again

Helping His people
Conquer many situations

Showing them that He was
And is, an omnipotent friend

And suddenly, with a burst of emotion,
Being stirred by the indwelling
Holy Ghost portion

Looking at the giant
Straight forward in his eyes

You are the defeated foe
She exclaimed, raising her sword
Of the spirit high

I do not have any doubt that
you, not I, shall be the one to die

The giant ran towards her
Ranting and waving and seething

Trying very hard to intimidate
Her into giving up and retreating

Still she stood still with a
Confident look on her face

No doubt or any expression of fear
Could any longer be traced

The giant, now very boisterous
And very much annoyed

Suddenly struck a blow to her head
But her helmet of salvation
Rendered it void

Still the giant persisted by
trying to pierce her with his sword

But she prevented him with her
Shield of faith, which, for every
Christian is one of God's
Impenetrable rewards

Spinning around, unexpectantly
To try and catch her off guard
The giant tried to punch her
In the chest but the breastplate of
Righteousness, once again, saved
Her from being destroyed

I'm shod with the preparation

Of the gospel and because of

This, now you know
That nothing you could ever
do could harm me

The word of God tells me so

Now there arose a violent wind
That knocked the giant
To the ground

And she ran and killed him with
The sword of the spirit
With a quick, strategic,
Overpowering sound

I am more than a conqueror
In Christ Jesus
She exclaimed as she
Completely realized

In Him I'll always win in
Every situation and always
Obtain the prize

Walk Before Me and Be Perfect

I listened to a message that
really changed my life
It ministered to my spirit
because it was such good advice

I will share it with you now
as someone declared it to me
I hope that it will, likewise
change your life and
truly set you free

I want to do the
best that I can
to live a perfect life
To walk in the ways of the
Lord and do the
things that are right

How can I live the
kind of life that God
expects me to
By yearning to faithfully
read His word and all of
His principles pursue

I'll need to let my light shine
everywhere I go
To think, talk and live
right, all of these
things just so

I'll be an effective witness
to everyone I meet
And help them to believe on
God's word and plainly
come to see

That living a perfect life in
God is a spiritual potentiality

Spare not! Cry aloud!
Lift up your voice
like a trumpet
I heard the Lord say
And this is a sound
principle that will cause
others to accept Him
into their lives each day

I'm meditating on the words
of God as a strong defense
mechanism for He said I'll
live in perfect peace if
I keep my mind on Him

I'm patterning my
lifestyle after Him
so that I will always have
Him in my life as a friend

Walk before me
and be perfect
I hear these words
again and again
I'm so blessed they
consistently run through
my mind helping me to avoid
a lifestyle of sin

Stumbling Block

They put a chair at the door
To block him in
But he knocked it down
And said that he would
Not continue to be
Imprisoned in sin

Someone closed the only
Window through which he
Could flee
But a fierce wind blew it
Open when he got on bended knee

Many words were used in an
Attempt to hold him back
But when he began to read the Bible
They became extremely slack

Someone tried to intimidate him
Every minute of the hour
But he rose above all of this
Confusion because he had been
Given God's saving power

In the end nothing could
Touch him
Nothing could do him
Any harm

Because finally instead of
Depending on himself
He stood back and let
God's amazing power
be performed

Lifting Up A Standard for Such A Time As This

Yes! We're lifting up a standard
With voices loud and clear
A perpetual resounding
So that everyone will hear

We will not become distracted
But will remain focused on our goals
So that nations will be won for the Lord
In our attempt to reach lost souls

We're witnessing such devastation
Daily, around the world
And with our spiritual eyes
That God has given to us
Know that these things must unfurl

God is calling to us, one and all
To choose right that we may live
No better decision could one
Ever make or advice
Could one ever give

How are we going to live right
You may ponder in your minds
By seeking God's help in every
Situation and all of Satan's
Tactics bind

Put on the breastplate of
Righteousness so that it will
Shield you and protect your heart
And of course you'll need the
Helmet of salvation so that with
The mind of Christ you'll never depart

The scriptures state it quite clearly
And it's not difficult to see
Stand fast therefore in the liberty
Wherein Christ has made you free

And be not entangled again
With the yoke of bondage
That's for you - it's for me

Can't you hear the trumpet blowing
Can't you feel the strong winds blow
Can't you see the Lord descending
Suspended in the heavenly billows

Only those that have accepted Him
As their personal Savior
Will be ready to go
Leaving this sinsick world behind
Them and all of their problems, so

Turn your face and your heart
To the Lord
Fall down on your knees and pray
Believe that Jesus was born to
Save you from an eternity
Of misery and dismay

Read your Bible daily
Fellowship with the Lord
Know that He is a faithful God
That will give everyone
A just reward

We will raise the banner high
And proclaim that Jesus'
Return is nigh

We will be faithful until death
Yes! Even with our dieing breath

We will not turn back or allow
Ourselves to be persuaded to
Walk in Satan's ways

Or listen to his wicked schemes
That causes us from God's
Word to sway

When anyone says yes to homosexuality
We will say, No!

Abortion, Drinking, Lieing, Cheating
No! No! No!

We are a royal priesthood
And our eternal future we will not risk

That's why we're lifting
Up a standard

For such a time as this!

About the Author

Carolyn Martin attended Rutgers University in Newark, New Jersey where she obtained her degree in Sociology. She continued her education at Kean College in Union, New Jersey where she received her Master's Degree in Elementary Education. She is married and has two children. Mrs. Martin works in the Orange Public School System where she teaches Elementary Education. She has worked in Orange for many years. She has always believed that positive words are profoundly important and that they outweigh negative ones overwhelmingly. She has used this strategy to motivate students to become socially stable individuals and academic achievers. She credits her positive attitude in life to her parents and the fact that they raised her up in church and taught her Godly principles. She began writing poetry many years ago when the school's music teacher gave an assignment to some of the students to create a rap. Realizing that so much negative rap was around at that time, Mrs. Martin decided to teach a positive one to the students. This rap, titled, "I Am the Best", was performed by three students as music was played in the background and the students did dance steps to it. This took place at the school's talent show. Subsequently, because of its positive words that encouraged students to meditate on doing what's right, to have confidence in themselves and to value their educational opportunities, the rap was coined the School's Pledge. To this day the students recite the School's Pledge daily, from grade kindergarten to grade six. Mrs. Martin has included the School's Pledge in this book for your enjoyment. This is the poem that served as a foundation of which birthed all of the other poems that were created by Carolyn Martin. She continues to write poetry, just about every day and hopes to have another book published in the future.

Breinigsville, PA USA
31 January 2010
231615BV00001B/98/A